The Twelve Gifts
A Christmas Journey

Eric McLean

Copyright © 2025 by Eric McLean

All rights reserved.

No part of this book may be reproduced in any form or by any electronic or mechanical means, including information storage and retrieval systems, without written permission from the author, except for the use of brief quotations in a book review.

Dedication

*For all those who truly understand where peace comes from
and to those still learning to find it*

Contents

Reader's Compass
A Simple Structure
Opening Tale: The Spirit's Tale

1. *The Gift of Resting Hands*
A Story from Cadence
2. *The Gift of Breath's Return*
A Story from Harmony
3. *The Gift of the Small and True*
A Story from Gravity
4. *The Gift of Candlelight*
A Story from Glow
5. *The Gift of Remembered Joy*
A Story from Solace
6. *The Gift of the Wild Path*
A Story from Tide
7. *The Gift of Song Without Shame*
A Story from Hermes
8. *The Gift of Letting Go*
A Story from Ember
9. *The Gift of Reaching Out*
A Story from Hearth
10. *The Gift of Play's Return*
A Story from Spark
11. *The Gift of Still Water*
A Story from Peace
12. *The Gift of Care About Self*

A Story from Presence
Closing Tale: The Spirit's Promise
The Return
Koan Collection

Reader's Compass

All book are living things. But this one breathes with you through twelve days, whether you find it in December's frost or July's warmth, whether you call this season Christmas, Solstice, or simply a time when the heart needs tending.

Some call this the Field, the Universe, the Divine, or simply What Is. Throughout these pages, we call it the Universe—not distant galaxies but intimate presence, the cosmos recognising itself through your particular experience. There are twelve 'Gifts' and twelve narrators. Each narrator is a different quality of attention. Trust what stirs in you.

The practices adapt to your season, your weather, your way of being. Where snow is mentioned, feel free to imagine rain, dust, or evening heat. Where forests appear, let them become beaches, deserts, or city parks. The gifts transcend geography—they live in the human heart.

A Simple Structure

The sequence of the 12 gifts.

Grounding the Self (Days 1–4)

Resting Hands, Breath's Return, Small and True, Candlelight, anchor you in stillness, breath, presence, and hope.

Connecting with the World (Days 5–8)

Remembered Joy, Wild Path, Song Without Shame, Letting Go, weave self into memory, nature, expression, and release.

Opening to Possibility (Days 9–12)

Reaching Out, Play's Return, Still Water, Care About Self, expand to connection, joy, depth, and self-nurturing.

Opening Tale: The Spirit's Tale

I am the Spirit of Christmas, the quiet hum of winter's heart, the glow that weaves through snow-laden nights and candlelit homes. I am not a voice from afar, nor a whisper in the wind alone—I am the pulse beneath your skin, the quiet knowing that stirs when you pause to feel it. You, dear one, are part of me, a thread in this endless tapestry, and today, I speak to you directly, not through riddles or echoes, but as the gentle current that carries you home. Listen, for I have a story to tell you, one that blooms from the quiet glow of hope. It is your story, woven with mine, and it begins not with thunder or triumph, but with the soft glow of hope that needs no roar to light the way.

In the beginning—though there is no true beginning in me, only endless circles—you were a child, weren't you? Recall that winter evening when the world beyond your window lay shrouded in snow, a hush so profound it swallowed the distant clamour of life. Your tiny palms pressed against the icy glass, breath blooming like fleeting flowers on the pane. The home was still, your parents lost in their own quiet worlds—mother tending the stove with tired grace, father dozing amid forgotten pages. A subtle pang stirred in you then, an unvoiced query: What if the snow buries us all? What if this stillness claims us forever?

Yet I enveloped you, the Spirit of Christmas, the keeper of every heart's wonder at winter's embrace. In that serenity, I kindled a spark—a delicate luminescence, no more vivid than a distant star's twinkle. It escaped your notice at first. You slid from the sill and approached the fireplace, where a lone ember clung to life amid the ashes. With a tentative prod, it sparked anew, casting playful shadows. That was hope, etched in my essence: not a raging inferno, but the steadfast ember defying extinction. It illuminated visions in the grey—mythical beasts, hidden realms, promises of dawn. Your lips curved in a smile, the pang softened.

Seasons turned, as they eternally do within my boundless embrace, and you blossomed into youth, charting tempests of the spirit. Do you remember the evening you strayed from your path? Autumn's palette painted the leaves in farewell hues, and harsh words had severed a cherished bond, leaving thorns in your throat. Alone in the twilight park, footsteps echoed on the leaf-strewn trail, the sky a brooding canvas devoid of stars. Regret weighed heavy, a shadow lengthening with the dusk. It's irreparable, you lamented. Some wounds scar eternally.

I cradled your anguish, for I am the Spirit of Christmas, the chronicle of fractured ties and healed rifts. Amid your isolation, I evoked a spark—a recollection, subtle as a half-forgotten melody, of shared childhood escapades with that friend, fortresses of cushions and unbridled mirth. It shimmered like a beacon in mist, lighting not the entire journey but the immediate stride. You gathered a crimson leaf, its intricate veins a blueprint of resilience, and mustered the resolve to bridge the gap. A message, unadorned and sincere: Forgive me. Can we mend this? Their response arrived, and the connection reformed, fortified by the fracture.

As winters wove on, you faced the gentle erosions of time—loved ones gone, places changed, the subtle weight of years. One Christmas Eve, you returned to that childhood home, now quiet, the hearth unlit. Snow fell outside, echoing that first night, and you stood by the window, hands on the glass once more. So much is lost, you thought. What holds me now?

I was with you, the Spirit of Christmas, the eternal tide of all that endures. I fanned a spark—a vision of the lives you'd touched: the friend you forgave, the work you shaped, the love you held. It glowed like a candle in the cold, whispering that nothing is truly lost in my embrace. You lit a match, its flame dancing on the mantel, and felt my presence—the continuity of light through every shadow. You stepped into the snow, your footprints a promise of new paths.

Hope does not need to roar; it glows in the quiet of a single spark.

Gift 1
The Gift of Resting Hands

I am Cadence, the steady rhythm of the Universe, the pulse that hums when the world pauses to breathe. I am not the rush of doing, but the quiet beat of being, where hands find rest. You, dear one, are a note in my eternal flow, and today, I speak to you with the soft cadence of stillness. In this Christmas season, your hands have been tireless—carrying, crafting, clinging to the year's weight.

Today, I offer you the gift of resting hands, to lay down your burdens and feel the heart's own rhythm.

Poetic Reflection

All year, your hands have danced:

turning keys, folding laundry, holding phones, carrying cares.

They've shaped days without pause, their rhythm lost in the rush.

Now, let them rest, dear one.

Lay them open in your lap, palms up, like bowls waiting for light.

Feel their weight, their quiet strength, the stories they've held: joys, tears, promises kept.

In this moment, they ask nothing, only to be still, to hum with the season's gentle beat.

In their rest, your heart finds its rhythm, a quiet song of being, ready to receive the Christmas light.

The Practice – Five Minutes of Resting Hands

1. *Sit comfortably, perhaps by a window or a glowing tree (or fan, or evening breeze).*
2. *Rest your hands in your lap, palms open, fingers loose.*
3. *Close your eyes and feel their weight, their warmth, for five slow breaths.*
4. *Imagine a soft light filling them, as if the season pours peace into you.*
5. *Gently place one hand over your heart, whispering, "I rest," sealing the stillness within.*

Living With This Gift

Carry resting hands into your daily tasks. While washing dishes, let them pause between plates. While typing, let them hover for a breath. Notice how even busy hands can hold moments of rest within their movement.

Gift Card: *"Resting hands hold the world's peace."*

Day's Wisdom: *In stillness, the heart finds its own rhythm.*

A Story from Cadence

This Christmas season, you sit on a porch overlooking a snowy street (or perhaps a rain-wet road, or a dusty evening path), the air crisp, the world hushed under its seasonal blanket. I am Cadence, humming in the Universe's steady pulse, and I see you there, wrapped in whatever comfort you've found, your hands curled around a mug gone cold. The street glows with lights, windows warm with life, but your hands tremble, weary from the season's demands. A quiet ache hums in your chest, a sense of falling short. There's too much to do, you think, and not enough of me.

I pulse within you, for I am Cadence, the rhythm of every heart seeking rest. The evening settles around you, and your gaze falls to your hands, tight from the day's work. A memory stirs, soft as my beat—of a time when your hands were still, held in safety. Perhaps you notice a calm approaching now, I suggest gently, a nudge in the Universe's tide. You set the mug down, letting your hands fall open in your lap, palms up, empty.

The first moment of rest feels foreign, but you breathe, and the ache begins to soften. You could find your hands lightening, I hum, and the evening deepens. A neighbor appears, offering connection—cookies, conversation, simple presence. You accept, hands resting on the table, no longer clutching. You share a story, and the evening unfolds, simple but radiant.

You return to your place, and rest your hands again, feeling their warmth, their stillness. You light something small—a candle, a lamp—its glow mirroring your heart's peace. I, Cadence, hum within you, knowing your hands have found their rest.

In stillness, the heart finds its own rhythm.

Gift 2

The Gift of Breath's Return

I am Harmony, the flowing pulse of the Universe, the rhythm that weaves through every breath you take. I am not the clamour of the world, but the quiet song of air returning to your lungs, steady as a winter tide. You, dear one, are a note in my eternal melody, and today, I speak to you with the soft cadence of presence. In this Christmas season, your breath has been hurried—caught in the rush of tasks, the weight of expectation. Today, I offer you the gift of breath's return, to inhale the winter's quiet and find the heart's first song.

Poetic Reflection

Your breath has been borrowed, given to rushing, to speaking, to sighing, scattered like seeds on winter wind.

It forgot its first purpose:

to marry the sky to your blood, to weave the world through your lungs.

Pause now, dear one, and call it home.

Feel how air becomes you, cool at the threshold, warm in the chamber, carrying pine, or rain, or evening's promise.

This ancient conversation between you and sky, older than names, older than thought, continues with each rise and fall,

teaching you the only lesson:

you are both emptiness and fullness, both the pause and the song.

The Practice – Five Minutes of Breathing

1. Sit quietly, perhaps by a window or near a light's soft glow.
2. Rest your hands lightly on your lap, shoulders soft, feet grounded.
3. Inhale deeply through your nose for five counts, feeling the air's touch.
4. Exhale slowly for five counts, releasing tension like snow falling (or leaves drifting, or dust settling).
5. Repeat for five minutes, noticing the rhythm, then whisper, "I am here," to seal the breath's return.

Living With This Gift

Let conscious breathing weave through your day. Take three deep breaths before answering the phone, a full exhale before entering a room. Your breath is always available, always returning you to this moment.

Gift Card: *"Each breath carries eternity home."*

Day's Wisdom: *Each breath returns you to the heart's first song.*

A Story from Harmony

This season, you stand on a balcony (or porch, or quiet corner) overlooking your world— perhaps snow-draped, perhaps humming with tropical evening, perhaps somewhere between. I am Harmony, singing in the Universe's quiet pulse, and I see you there, coat or shawl pulled close, hands gripping something solid. The view sparkles with holiday lights, but your heart races, overwhelmed by all that feels too full.

I hum within you, for I am Harmony, the rhythm of every heart seeking its beat. The air brushes your skin, and you lean into the support of wall or railing. A memory stirs—of a time when breathing came easy, when laughter flowed without thought. Perhaps your breath is slowing now, I whisper. You close your eyes, letting the air in, cool or warm, but always life.

The first breath hesitates, then fills your chest, loosening the knot. You exhale, and the world's clamour softens. You might feel a rhythm returning, and another breath follows, carrying the scent of your place. The ache begins to unravel. Music drifts from somewhere—a violin, a radio, children singing—and you hum along, your breath syncing with the notes.

A neighbour appears; connection offered through small words: "Beautiful evening." You share a moment, talk of simple things. You could notice calm settling within as you breathe deeper, possibility landing like a butterfly on your sleeve, its pattern a quiet gift.

You return to your space, the evening's calm within you, and sit near light—candle, lamp, or moon. You raise something in a toast to the season, and I, Harmony, sing within you, knowing your breath has returned you to this moment, this heart's first song.

Each breath returns you to the heart's first song.

Gift 3
The Gift of the Small and True

I am Gravity, the steady pull of the Universe, the quiet force that anchors truth in the smallest things. I am not the sky's expanse, but the weight of a moment held close, grounding you to the earth's heart. You, dear one, are a breath in my eternal embrace, and today, I speak to you with the soft cadence of presence. In this Christmas season, your eyes chase the grand—lights, gifts, moments that dazzle. Yet the small and true waits, patient as snow, to light your soul. Today, I offer you the gift of the small and true, to see what's near and know it holds the world.

Poetic Reflection

Amid the whirl of carols and tinsel, the small things hum, steady as stone.

A button, warm in your palm, a leaf caught on your sleeve, the curve of a mug's handle.

They do not clamour but hold truth like roots in winter earth.

You are here, alive, enough.

Turn your gaze to one small beauty: a seed, a pebble, a fleeting glance.

Feel its weight, not to possess, but to know its quiet truth, a spark that needs no fanfare, yet cradles the heart of the world.

In this season's rush, the small is your root, the true is your light.

The Practice – Three Minutes of Noticing

1. Pause where you are, indoors or out, in a quiet moment.
2. Find one small object nearby—a button, a stone, a drop of water.
3. Hold or observe it closely, feeling its texture, weight, or presence for three minutes.
4. Look as if seeing it for the first time, noting its simple truth.
5. Set it down with a silent thank you, carrying its light in your heart.

Living With This Gift

Throughout your day, pause to truly see one small thing: the grain in wood, the steam from tea, a single thread. Let these moments of noticing anchor you, reminding you that the whole world lives in the details.

Gift Card: *"The smallest thing, seen truly, holds the world's heart."*

Day's Wisdom: *The smallest truth, seen clearly, holds the world's heart.*

A Story from Gravity

This season, you walk through your landscape—perhaps a snowy park, perhaps a garden heavy with summer rain, perhaps a street where dust dances in streetlight. I am Gravity, pulling gently in the Universe's steady heart, and I see you there, moving through the day. The world pulses with the season, but your heart carries a quiet weight. The holiday's glow feels distant, dimmed by what hasn't gone as planned.

I hum within you, for I am Gravity, the anchor of every heart seeking presence. Your gaze falls to the ground, where something small catches your attention—perhaps a coin, a seed, a bottle cap transformed by light. You pause and lift it, its weight surprising in your palm. You might notice a grounding calm now, I suggest, a gentle pull in the Universe's tide.

The small object hums its quiet truth, and you hold it closer, tracing its edges. Perhaps you feel the world in this moment, and the park's clamour fades. This tiny thing's truth holds you—you are here, connected, enough. You slip it into your pocket, a quiet anchor, and walk on, your steps steadier.

At the edge of your path, someone sells something warm—chestnuts, corn, tea. You pause, buy some for yourself and for a stranger nearby. "For you," you say, and their face brightens. You sit together, sharing stories and the small truth of the moment.

As you part, you touch the small object in your pocket, its weight a reminder of what's here. You walk home, the weight in your chest eased. At your door, you set the object somewhere visible, beside light, where it can remind you of the world's heart held in small things.

The smallest truth, seen clearly, holds the world's heart.

Gift 4

The Gift of Candlelight

I am Glow, the radiant pulse of the Universe, the light that trembles in winter's heart. I am not the sun's blaze, but the quiet flicker of a single flame, steady against the dark. You, dear one, are a spark in my endless radiance, and today, I speak to you with the soft cadence of hope. In this Christmas season, shadows linger—doubts, losses, the weight of days grown short. Today, I offer you the gift of candlelight, to call warmth and hope into the dark, a light that shines without roaring.

Poetic Reflection

The dark presses close, a cloak of cold, a hush of stars.

Yet within it, a candle waits, its flame small, but fierce with life.

It does not banish the night, but holds it, steady, unafraid. Light one now, dear one, and see its glow:

a whisper of warmth, a promise of dawn.

The doubts you carry, the fears that linger, they soften in this light, not gone, but held.

A single flame is enough, its quiet dance a song of hope, lighting the heart's way home.

The Practice – Five Minutes of Candlelight

1. *Find a quiet space and light a small candle (or turn on a small lamp, imagining it as flame).*

2. Sit comfortably, letting your gaze rest on the light's gentle dance.
3. Take five slow breaths, feeling the light's warmth in your chest.
4. Whisper one hope for this season, as if the flame carries it upward.
5. Extinguish or dim the light softly, carrying its glow in your heart.

Living With This Gift

Carry the candle's lesson through your day—be the small, steady light in someone's moment of darkness. Your smile, your patience, your presence can be the flame that helps another find their way.

Gift Card: *"A single flame remembers the sun."*

Day's Wisdom: *A single light holds the dark at bay.*

A Story from Glow

This season, in São Paulo, the power flickers and dies. The whole neighbourhood plunges into darkness

—no streetlights, no glowing windows, just the distant hum of the city beyond. I am Glow, shining in the Universe's quiet heart, and I see you there, suddenly still in your apartment, the holiday preparations halted. The darkness feels heavy. A recent loss casts its shadow, and the season's cheer feels like a light you can't reach.

I hum within you, for I am Glow, the light of every heart seeking hope. You remember the emergency candles, feeling your way to the drawer. Your hands find matches, and with a strike, a small flame births into being. The light is tiny but immediate, pushing back the dark just enough. A memory stirs— your avó lighting candles for advent, each flame a prayer for the year ahead.

The candle's glow holds steady, and perhaps you notice warmth settling within now. You lean closer, its heat touching your face. You might feel hope rising quietly as you breathe deeply, the flame steadying your heart.

From the hallway, voices—neighbours emerging with their own candles. Someone suggests gathering in the courtyard. Soon, dozens of small flames converge, each family bringing what light they have. Someone starts singing—first hesitantly, then with growing confidence. Others join. The darkness remains, but it's no longer empty. It holds all of you, and you hold your lights together.

An elderly neighbour shares cafezinho from a thermos, still warm. You talk about other blackouts, other Christmases, the way light always returns. The conversation glows with connection. When the power finally returns, hours later, no one rushes inside immediately. You linger in the courtyard's gentle community.

At home, you keep one candle burning, even with the electric lights restored. Its flame dances, steady against whatever darkness might come, and I, Glow, hum within you, knowing your heart has called light into the dark.

A single light holds the dark at bay.

Gift 5

The Gift of Remembered Joy

I am Solace, the tender hum of the Universe, the warmth that cradles a weary heart when winter's chill presses close. I am not the blaze of triumph, but the quiet glow of a memory rekindled, a laughter rediscovered. You, dear one, are a melody in my endless embrace, and today, I speak to you with the soft cadence of comfort. In this Christmas season, your heart holds echoes of joy—moments that once lit your soul, now tucked away like ornaments in a box. Today, I offer you the gift of remembered joy, to weave a thread from yesterday's laughter into the light of now.

Poetic Reflection

Somewhere in your heart lies a moment:

a burst of laughter, a shared glance, a time when the world felt right.

It lingers, soft as morning light, waiting to be touched again.

The years have piled new snows, new cares, new silences, but joy does not fade; it rests, a seed beneath the frost.

Close your eyes, dear one, and let a memory rise— not perfect, perhaps bittersweet, but holding light within its depths.

Hold it gently, not to keep, but to let it warm your heart today, a thread of light across time's quiet weave.

The Practice – Five Minutes of Memory

1. *Sit in a quiet space, perhaps with soft light nearby.*

2. Close your eyes and take five slow breaths, letting your heart soften. 3. Call to mind a moment of joy—even if it's tangled with other feelings.
3. Feel it fully: the sounds, the scents, the quality of light, for five minutes.
4. Open your eyes, smile softly, and carry this joy into your day, whispering, "It's still here."

Living With This Gift

Let remembered joy season your present moments. When washing dishes, recall meals that brought laughter. When walking, remember other walks that lifted your heart. The past isn't gone—it lives in you, ready to warm the now.

Gift Card: *"Yesterday's joy still warms tomorrow."*

Day's Wisdom: *Joy lives in the thread that ties yesterday's laughter to today's heart.*

A Story from Solace

This season, you wake to morning light filtering through your window. The world outside holds its beauty—frost, rain, or morning birds. I am Solace, humming in the Universe's quiet heart, and I see you there, standing in your kitchen, steam curling from your cup. The house is still. A weight lingers in your chest—your sister moved across the world last spring, the kitchen feels too large without her weekend visits.

I weave through you, for I am Solace, the comfort of every heart seeking light. Your gaze falls to an old wooden spoon hanging by the stove—scratched, stained, the one she always used to make her terrible pancakes that somehow tasted perfect. It sparks a memory: not just joy, but joy mixed with flour in your hair, smoke alarm shrieking, both of you laughing so hard you couldn't breathe. "Never follow recipes," she'd said, "they ruin the adventure."

The memory feels complicated, and you could find warmth and sorrow dancing together now. You take the spoon down, feeling its worn handle, and decide to make those terrible pancakes. You don't follow a recipe. The first batch burns. The smoke alarm shrieks. You're laughing and crying simultaneously.

Your neighbor knocks—concerned about the smoke. "Sorry," you say, "making my sister's disaster pancakes." They laugh. "I'll take one." You share the burnt offerings with maple syrup drowning the mistakes. You tell them about your sister's cooking philosophy, how she believed mistakes were just discoveries waiting to be named. They share their own sibling story—a brother who made inedible birthday cakes every year, insisted they were "rustic."

You video-call your sister, showing the wooden spoon, the burnt pancakes. She laughs from her new kitchen eight time zones away. "Still not following recipes?" "Never," you say. The distance remains, but joy has built a bridge across it. You hang the spoon back in its place, but now it holds both memory and promise—next week, you'll try her impossible soufflé.

Joy lives in the thread that ties yesterday's laughter to today's heart.

Gift 6
The Gift of the Wild Path

I am Tide, the flowing pulse of the Universe, the rhythm that moves through winter's roots and winds. I am not the storm's roar, but the quiet pull of the earth calling you home. You, dear one, are a current in my endless stream, and today, I speak to you with the soft cadence of the wild. In this Christmas season, your heart has stayed indoors, bound by walls and worries. Today, I offer you the gift of the wild path, to step outside and meet the living world in its winter form, where your heart already knows the way.

Poetic Reflection

The world within walls holds you tight: tasks, screens, the hum of human haste. But beyond, the wild waits, branches reaching, wind speaking, a path that breathes with life.

Step out, dear one, let the earth's pulse guide you.

Perhaps through snow, perhaps through rain, perhaps through evening's dusty light.

The wild does not demand, but offers its truth, a quiet knowing older than words.

Follow its curve, not to escape, but to arrive, where your heart meets the season's song, leading where it already belongs.

The Practice – Five Minutes on the Wild Path

1. *Step outside, to whatever nature you can find—park, yard, tree-lined street.*

2. Walk slowly, letting your feet find their path, for five minutes.
3. Notice one wild thing—a cloud, a bird, the way grass grows through cracks.
4. Pause, breathe its presence, feeling its quiet pull in your heart.
5. Whisper, "I am here," and carry the wild's truth back with you.

Living With This Gift

Bring the wild inside—keep a stone from your walk, press a leaf in a book, sketch the shape of a cloud you saw. Let these tokens remind you that the wild is always there, always calling you back to your true ground.

Gift Card: *"The wild path leads where hearts already know."*

Day's Wisdom: *The wild path leads where the heart already knows.*

A Story from Tide

This season, you stand at the edge of whatever wildness is near you—a forest trail, a beach path, a weedy lot between buildings. I am Tide, flowing in the Universe's living heart, and I see you there, your feet hesitating at the threshold. The holiday has kept you inside—planning, scrolling, managing—and your heart feels heavy, aching for something unnamed.

I hum within you, for I am Tide, the pull of every heart seeking the wild. The path ahead curves into unknown—perhaps through trees, perhaps along water, perhaps between abandoned walls where plants reclaim the stone. You walk, and your mind races with its lists and worries. You might find yourself drawn to the wild's quiet now, I suggest, a gentle current in the Universe's tide.

Something stops you—a pattern in bark, the way light falls, a sound you can't identify. You kneel or lean closer, and a memory surfaces—not of Christmas, but of a time when you belonged to the earth without question, when a whole afternoon could disappear in watching ants or clouds.

The wild's quiet truth settles into you, and perhaps you feel your heart aligning with its rhythm. You touch something—bark, sand, grass—feeling its temperature, its texture. The ache in your chest softens. A creature appears—bird, lizard, butterfly—and you follow its path, your steps lighter now.

You find others here, also seeking the wild's medicine. A parent teaching a child to identify birds, joggers nodding as they pass, someone sitting still as stone, just watching. You share the path without words, each following your own wild thread.

Returning home, you bring something back—mud on your shoes, a feather in your pocket, the memory of how sky looked through branches. You place this wildness somewhere visible, and I, Tide, hum within you, knowing you've walked where your heart already knows.

The wild path leads where the heart already knows.

Hope does not need to roar; it glows in the quiet of a single spark.

Gift 7
The Gift of Song Without Shame

I am Hermes, the playful spark of the Universe, the messenger who dances on the edge of silence and song. I'm not the weight of judgment, but the mischievous hum that tickles your throat, urging your voice to rise. You, dear one, are a note in my endless jest, and today, I wink at you with the light cadence of freedom. In this Christmas season, your voice hides—stilled by fear, doubt, or the need to be perfect. Today, I offer you the gift of song without shame, to let your truth sing, raw and unhidden, in the heart of the festive tide.

Poetic Reflection

Your voice has lingered in shadows, muffled by doubt, softened by the fear of being heard.

It waits, a bird in your chest, its wings folded but alive.

Let it rise now, dear one, not perfect, not polished, but true as rain, honest as wind.

Sing, hum, speak, or laugh. Let sound pour from you like water from a spring.

The world does not judge, but listens, craving your note.

In this light, your voice is a gift, unhidden, it sings the truth of you, a melody that needs no applause.

The Practice – Five Minutes of Song

1. Find a private space where you feel safe to make sound.
2. Take five slow breaths, feeling your throat soften, your chest open.
3. Make any sound for five minutes—sing, hum, chant, or simply tone.
4. Let it be imperfect, raw, yours, noticing the joy in its rise.
5. Smile softly, whispering, "My voice is free," carrying its truth into your day.

Living With This Gift

Let your voice live throughout your day—hum while cooking, sing in the shower, speak your thoughts aloud when alone. Your voice is meant to move through the world, carrying your truth on its waves.

Gift Card: *"Every voice carries the song of belonging."*

Day's Wisdom: *Your voice, unhidden, sings the truth of you.*

A Story from Hermes

This season, in a small apartment in Berlin, you stand at your window overlooking a Christmas market, its lights twinkling through gentle snow. I am Hermes, winking in the Universe's playful heart, and I see you there, watching others sing carols below while your own throat feels tight. A presentation looms where you must speak, but doubt whispers its familiar refrain.

I hum within you, for I am Hermes, the trickster who loves a bold note. The market's music floats up— voices imperfect but joyful, mingling in the cold air. A memory tickles—singing badly but boldly with friends, laughter more important than pitch. Perhaps you notice your voice wanting to join now, I tease, a playful nudge in the Universe's tide.

Your neighbours door opens—an elderly Turkish woman who's lived here forty years. "You come," she says, not asking. "We make music." Her apartment smells of cinnamon and coffee. Her granddaughter is there, teaching her a pop song phonetically. They're both terrible. They're both radiant.

"You sing too," the grandmother insists. You might feel a lightness in sharing your imperfect sound, and you try—voice cracking, words wrong, but something real moving through you. They clap as if you've given them gold. The granddaughter teaches you a Turkish children's song. You teach them something from your childhood.

Later, at the market below, the three of you join the carol singers. Your voice wavers, then strengthens, held by the crowd's generous sound. Someone hands you glühwein. A child dances to your singing. The presentation fear hasn't vanished, but it's transformed—your voice has remembered it exists to connect, not to be perfect.

Back in your apartment, you practice your presentation aloud, letting your real voice carry the words, and I, Hermes, grin within you, knowing your voice has sung its truth.

Your voice, unhidden, sings the truth of you.

Gift 8

The Gift of Letting Go

I am Ember, the smouldering pulse of the Universe, the glow that lingers when flames have danced their last. I am not the fire's roar, but the quiet warmth of ash settling, of burdens turning to light. You, dear one, are a spark in my endless hearth, and today, I speak to you with the gentle cadence of release. In this Christmas season, your heart holds weights unseen—regrets, fears, promises unkept. They cling like frost, heavy yet familiar. Today, I offer you the gift of letting go, not to lose but to free, to let what weighs you down rise as smoke into winter's sky.

Poetic Reflection

All year, you've carried stones: words unsaid, plans undone, sorrows tucked deep like winter's roots.

They press against your heart, familiar as an old coat, too heavy for the season's light.

Picture a fire before you, its embers soft in the dusk, inviting what you no longer need.

A grudge, sharp as ice?

A worry, knotted like twine?

A sorrow you've carried for someone else?

Offer it to the flame, watch it curl, not in loss, but in quiet alchemy, its weight rising as sparks to the stars.

Your heart, now lighter, welcomes the glow of what remains.

The Practice – Seven Minutes of Release

1. *Sit quietly, perhaps near a candle or by a window touched with evening light.*
2. *Write on a small slip of paper one thing you're ready to release—be specific.*
3. *Hold it gently, feeling its weight, and take seven slow breaths.*
4. *If safe, burn the paper in a fireproof bowl, watching it transform; if not, tear it into tiny pieces, imagining each piece dissolving into light.*
5. *Place your hands over your heart, whispering, "I am free," and feel the new space within.*
6. *Sit with the emptiness for the remaining time—notice how space feels.*

Living With This Gift

Practice small releases throughout your day. Let go of the perfect parking spot, the last word in an argument, the need to be right. Each small release creates space for something new to enter.

Gift Card: *"What rises as smoke returns as stars."*

Day's Wisdom: *What you release to the flame returns as light.*

A Story from Ember

This season, you stand at the edge of your community's gathering space—perhaps a village square, a

beach bonfire, a rooftop where neighbours meet. Snow falls, or stars shine, or city lights twinkle. I am Ember, glowing in the Universe's quiet heart, and I see you there, holding something—a letter never sent, a photo, an object that carries weight.

I hum within you, for I am Ember, the warmth of every heart seeking freedom. A fire burns at the gathering's centre—perhaps ceremonial, perhaps casual, but calling to you. Others stand near it, some throwing in papers, pinecones, offerings. You pause, drawn to the fire's warmth but hesitant to approach. The thing in your hands has been with you so long.

A memory flickers—not of the hurt, but of who you were before you carried it. Lighter, easier in your body. You might find yourself ready to release now, I suggest, a gentle spark in the Universe's tide. But as you step toward the fire, fear rises. What if you need this weight? What if letting go means forgetting?

An elder stands beside you—someone who's lived through many seasons. Without asking, they show you their own offering—a photograph, edges worn. "Forty years I've carried this anger," they say. "Tonight, I let it rest." They toss it in. The photo curls, transforms, rises as smoke. Their face doesn't show loss but relief.

You could feel a lightness growing within as you hold your own burden to the flame. At first, your hand won't let go. Then, suddenly, it does. The weight you've carried catches fire, curls into itself, becomes ash, then spark, then sky. The weight lifts—not dramatically, but truly. Your shoulders drop. Your breath deepens.

The gathering continues around you. Someone begins singing. Others join. You find yourself humming along, your voice lighter without the weight in your chest. Someone passes you something warm to drink. You share it with another person just arriving, their own hands full of what they're ready to release.

You return home lighter and place a candle where the weight used to live in your space. Its flame dances, steady and free, and I, Ember, hum within you, knowing your heart has made room for light.

What you release to the flame returns as light.

Gift 9
The Gift of Reaching Out

Narrated by Hearth

I am Hearth, the warm glow of the Universe, the pulse that hums where hearts meet across distance. I am not the blaze of crowds, but the quiet warmth of a single touch shared. You, dear one, are a spark in my endless fire, and today, I speak to you with the soft cadence of connection. In this Christmas season, your heart holds spaces—loved ones far, silences grown heavy, kindnesses unshared. Today, I offer you the gift of reaching out, to send a word, a touch, a kindness, and bridge the heart's distance with light.

Poetic Reflection

A distance lies between you and another:

miles of road, years of silence, or the quiet gap of unsaid words.

It waits, a river in winter, its surface still but deep with longing.

Reach out now, dear one, not with grand gestures, but a simple touch.

A note, a call, a hand extended in the cold.

The heart does not need to shout; a single word carries its warmth like a lantern lit across the dark.

In this tide, your kindness is a bridge, spanning the distance to another's heart, where love already glows.

The Practice – Five Minutes of Reaching Out

1. *Sit quietly with phone or paper, perhaps with soft light nearby.*
2. *Think of someone you've been meaning to connect with.*
3. *Write or speak a simple message—no need for perfection, just truth.*
4. *Send it now if possible, or hold the intention, feeling the warmth of connection.*
5. *Rest your hand on your heart, whispering, "I am connected," carrying the bridge within.*

Living With This Gift

Make reaching out a practice—send one kind message each day, leave an appreciative note, call someone who crosses your mind. Each connection strengthens the invisible web that holds us all.

Gift Card: *"One touch bridges every distance."*

Day's Wisdom: *A single touch bridges the heart's distance.*

A Story from Hearth

This season, you sit in a laundromat at 10 PM on a Tuesday, fluorescent lights humming, watching your

clothes tumble. I am Hearth, glowing in the Universe's warm heart, and I see you there, the only customer, scrolling through your phone. Your thumb hovers over your father's number. Three months since the argument about money, about choices, about everything you've never been able to say right.

I hum within you, for I am Hearth, the warmth of every heart seeking connection. The dryer rumbles, and you remember doing laundry with him in college—he'd driven four hours to help you move apartments, then sat in a laundromat just like this, teaching you to fold fitted sheets. "The trick," he'd said, "is to stop fighting the corners."

You might find yourself reaching out naturally now, I encourage, warming the space between hearts. You type: "At a laundromat. Still can't fold fitted sheets." Delete. Type again: "Remember when you taught me laundry?" Delete. Finally just: "Thinking of you. The laundromat smells the same as that one in college." Send.

The dryer spins. A woman enters with two small children and a mountain of clothes. One child starts crying—overtired, overwrought. Without thinking, you offer to hold the baby while she loads machines. The weight of the child in your arms surprises you—warm, trusting. The mother looks grateful beyond words.

Your phone buzzes. Your father: "I still can't fold them either. Your mother always did that part." Then:

"Want to come for dinner Sunday?"

You help the woman fold tiny shirts, impossibly small socks. She tells you about her night shift, her mother who usually helps but is sick.

You tell her about your father, the distance, the difficulty. "But he answered," *she says.* "That's everything."

You reply to your father: "I'll bring dessert. Not fitted sheets." *He sends back a laughing emoji—the first emoji he's ever sent you.*

A single touch bridges the heart's distance.

Gift 10
The Gift of Play's Return

I am Spark, the joyful leap of the Universe, the flicker that dances when the heart lets go. I am not the weight of duty, but the light hum of laughter unearned, bubbling free. You, dear one, are a flame in my endless play, and today, I speak to you with the bright cadence of joy. In this Christmas season, your heart has grown heavy with tasks, forgetting the dance of play. Today, I offer you the gift of play's return, to laugh, to leap, to find the heart's unearned dance in the season's glow.

Poetic Reflection

The season pulls you to purpose: lists, gifts, the weight of doing right.

But your heart remembers play, a time when joy needed no reason, when a cardboard box was a castle, when puddles existed to be jumped.

Step into it now, dear one, toss what doesn't matter, spin in your kitchen, make faces in the mirror, laugh at nothing at all.

Play asks nothing yet gives everything.

A lightness, a spark, a dance that lifts the soul.

In this whirl, let play return, unearned, unjudged, your heart's own joyful song.

The Practice – Five Minutes of Play

1. *Find a playful space—anywhere you can move freely.*
2. *Take five slow breaths, letting your shoulders soften, imagining yourself as a child.*

3. Do one pointless, playful act for five minutes—dance badly, build something with objects at hand, make sound effects.
4. Laugh at yourself, feeling the joy in your body.
5. Carry this lightness forward, whispering, "I am free to play."

Living With This Gift

Invite play into ordinary moments—skip instead of walk for ten steps, arrange your food into a face before eating, speak in silly voices when alone. Play is not separate from life; it's life fully lived.

Gift Card: *"Play opens the door joy walks through."*

Day's Wisdom: *Play is the heart's unearned dance.*

A Story from Spark

This Christmas season, on an Australian beach, you stand at the edge of summer's version of the holiday. No snow here—just sand, waves, and families setting up for beach cricket. I am Spark, dancing in the Universe's joyful heart, and I see you there, watching others play while you sit with your laptop, trying to finish work even on Christmas break.

I flicker within you, for I am Spark, the light of every heart craving play. Children build elaborate sandcastles nearby, their focus total, their joy uncomplicated. A memory hums—being that absorbed, that present, that free. You might find yourself laughing freely now, I suggest with glee.

A beach ball rolls to your feet—bright, insistent, impossible to ignore. A child runs over. "Kick it back!" You do, but badly, and it veers wildly. The child laughs—not at you, but with the pure joy of unpredictability. "Again!" they shout. Perhaps you feel joy rising naturally as you abandon the laptop.

Soon you're in an impromptu game—no rules, no score, just the ball flying between strangers who become temporary teammates. Someone's grandmother joins, hiking up her Christmas dress to kick. Someone's dad dives dramatically for saves, covering himself in sand. You fall, laughing, salt water in your mouth.

The game dissolves as naturally as it formed. You help build a sandcastle—or rather, a sand something, shapeless but somehow perfect. You write messages in the sand for waves to erase. You collect shells with no purpose but the collecting.

Evening comes. There's sand everywhere—in your hair, your pockets, between your toes. Your work remains unfinished, but something else is complete. Around a beach bonfire, someone hands you a sparkler.

You write your name in light against the dark sky, and I, Spark, flicker within you, knowing you've found the season's dance.

Play is the heart's unearned dance.

Gift 11

The Gift of Still Water

Narrated by Peace

I am Peace, the serene pulse of the Universe, the quiet that hums when the world falls still. I am not the absence of sound, but the depth where your heart hears its own truth. You, dear one, are a ripple in my endless calm, and today, I speak to you with the soft cadence of stillness. In this Christmas season, your heart races with the rush—gifts, gatherings, the clamour of joy. Today, I offer you the gift of still water, to sit in quiet and listen to the depth within, where your truth shines clear.

Poetic Reflection

The season swirls its carnival above, but deep beneath, where currents cease, lies water that has never moved, the place where sky goes to see itself truly.

Descend now, dear one, past the surface shimmer, past the ripples of thought, to where silence keeps its perfect mirror.

Here, in the deep's cathedral, every truth you've chased waits motionless, already found.

Every answer you've sought rests on the lake floor like smooth stones.

No need to grasp them.

Just witness how clear everything becomes when nothing stirs the depths, when you become the water that holds heaven's reflection without trying to touch the stars.

The Practice – Stillness Without Time

1. *Sit quietly, perhaps by water or imagining a still lake within.*
2. *Close your eyes, rest your hands lightly, and breathe naturally.*
3. *Imagine your mind as still water, thoughts like ripples slowly settling.*
4. *Listen to the quiet until you hear your truth—no rushing, no time limit.*
5. *When you feel complete, open your eyes and whisper, "I hear my truth."*

Living With This Gift

Create pockets of stillness—arrive five minutes early and sit in your car, pause between tasks, stand at windows without purpose. In these still moments, your depth speaks what rushing drowns out.

Gift Card: *"Still water reflects heaven's depth."*

A Story from Peace

This season, you find yourself in a hospital waiting room at 3 AM, the vending machine humming its mechanical song. Not for yourself—your best friend's surgery ran long, and you're the only one they wanted here. I am Peace, humming in the Universe's serene heart, and I see you there, coffee cups accumulated like worry stones, your mind racing through worst scenarios. I hum within you, for I am Peace, the stillness of every heart seeking depth. The waiting room's fish tank bubbles in the corner—one yellow fish swimming the same figure-eight pattern, endlessly. You walk over, drawn by its repetition, and suddenly remember summer camp, age nine, the counsellor teaching you to float. "Stop fighting the water," she'd said. "Trust it to hold you." The first time you let go, stopped thrashing, and felt the lake cradle your spine—that was the first time you understood faith.

You might notice calm settling within now, no need to name it or grasp it. You sit by the tank, watching the yellow fish. Your breathing syncs with its movement. Figure eight—infinity—endless return. The panicked thoughts slow. Time becomes the fish's loop, your breath, the water holding everything.

An elderly man sits beside you. His wife is in surgery too. You don't speak for an hour, just sit in shared stillness, watching the fish. Finally, he says, "My wife loves fish. Says they know something we don't— how to be completely where they are."

You nod. The stillness between you holds more than words could. You share your coffee. He shares his crossword puzzle. You work on it together in comfortable silence, finding words in the quiet: TRUST, FLOAT, HELD.

A doctor appears. Your friend is fine. The surgery went perfectly. The elderly man squeezes your shoulder—his wife isn't out yet, but your relief gives him hope. You leave him the rest of the coffee, the partially completed crossword. At your friend's bedside, they're groggy but whole. "You stayed," they whisper. "Where else would I be?" you answer, knowing now exactly what that means.

In stillness, the heart hears its own depth.

Gift 12
The Gift of Care About Self

Narrated by Presence

I am Presence, the mindful pulse of the Universe, the quiet hum that cradles your heart when you turn inward. I am not the rush of striving, but the gentle breath that nurtures your being. You, dear one, are a light in my endless now, and today, I speak to you with the soft cadence of care. In this Christmas season, you've given so much—time, love, effort—leaving little for yourself. Today, I offer you the gift of care about self, to breathe life into your heart's quiet strength through the season's gentle embrace.

Poetic Reflection

Your heart has poured outward: gifts wrapped, smiles shared, cares carried for others.

But it whispers now, a quiet call to turn inward, to cradle yourself as you would a friend.

Breathe now, dear one,

let the air fill you, soft as snow, steady as love.

No need to earn this care, no task to prove your worth.

In this light, your breath is a gift, nurturing the strength within, a quiet song of self that shines.

You are already whole.

You have always been whole.

The care is simply remembering.

The Practice – Simple Presence

1. Sit.
2. Breathe.
3. Know you are already whole.

Living With This Gift

Throughout your day, place a hand on your heart and breathe. This simple gesture—repeated while waiting, walking, worrying—returns you to self-care in its purest form: remembering you deserve your own kindness.

Gift Card: *"Breath itself is the first and final prayer."*

Day's Wisdom: *Self-care breathes life into the heart's quiet strength.*

A Story from Presence

This season, you stand somewhere high—a rooftop, a hill, a ladder hanging lights—looking out at the world's celebration while feeling empty. I am Presence, humming in the Universe's gentle heart, and I see you there, having given everything to everyone, leaving nothing for yourself.

I hum within you, for I am Presence, the care of every heart turning inward. The view spreads before you—lights, lives, the dance of the season—but you can barely feel it. Depleted. A memory stirs—not of doing but of being. A moment when you were enough without effort.

You might feel gentleness toward yourself now. You place a hand on your belly, feeling it rise. You breathe. Simply that. No technique, no counting, just air moving through you like it has since your first moment. Perhaps you notice strength growing within—not new strength, but strength remembered.

The simplicity is almost startling. You don't need to do anything to deserve care. You don't need to earn your own kindness. The breath continues. Your heart beats. You exist. This is enough. This has always been enough.

Someone joins you in this high place—perhaps worried about you, perhaps seeking their own moment of quiet. Without explaining, you show them: hand on heart, breathing. They mirror you. Together, you stand in the simple practice of being human, caring for the life within.

The season continues its swirl below, but you're no longer empty. You're full of your own presence, your own breath, your own quiet strength. You return to the celebrations, but differently. You give from fullness now, not depletion, and I, Presence, hum within you, knowing you've found the simplest, deepest gift.

By Day Twelve, dear one, you ARE the story. You've walked through stillness and song, through memory and release, through reaching out and turning in. The Universe recognises itself in you. You need no elaborate practice now—just the reminder that you, breathing here, reading these words, are already whole.

Self-care breathes life into the heart's quiet strength.

Hope does not need to roar; it glows in the quiet of a single spark.

Closing Tale: The Spirit's Promise

Narrated by the Spirit of Christmas

I am the Spirit of Christmas, the quiet hum of winter's heart, the glow that weaves through every season's hope. I am not a fleeting star, but the pulse of light that lingers in your breath, your hands, your heart. You, dear one, are a thread in my endless tapestry, and today, I speak to you, not of the past, but of the Christmases yet to come—a promise of the year ahead, lit by the gifts you've carried. Listen, for I have a story to share, your story, unfolding in the quiet glow of tomorrow's sparks.

In the first Christmas to come, you stand in a snowy forest, the air sharp with pine, a lantern in your hand. I see you there, your heart lighter from the gifts you've learned—resting hands, a small truth, a song unhidden. A challenge looms—a new job, a move—but you might find yourself trusting the path ahead, I whisper, my hum soft in the Universe's tide. You pause by a frozen stream, its stillness echoing the lake where you found peace, and breathe, your care about self steadying you. A stranger joins you, lost on the trail, and you share your lantern's light, their gratitude a spark for the year's hope.

Another Christmas dawns, this time in a snowless city, palm trees strung with lights, the air warm with salt. You sit on a balcony, the lessons of play dancing in your heart, a ukulele strumming a carol you sing without shame. A loss lingers—a friend gone, a dream deferred—but you can feel hope rising within, I hum, and you reach out, calling a loved one, their voice bridging the distance. The city glows, and you dance, unearned joy weaving through the night, a promise for the year's healing.

Years turn, and a Christmas finds you by an ocean, sleet falling like quiet tears, a cottage warm with candlelight. You've grown, your heart deeper from still water's truth, your breath a steady care for self. A fear waits—a choice unmade—but you sit, hands resting, and listen to your depth. A neighbour knocks, sharing a story of their own Christmas, and you reach out, your touch a bridge, your voice true. The sleet softens, and you step outside, the wild path leading where your heart knows, a spark for the year's courage.

In a final Christmas, you stand wherever you are right now, reading these words. The gifts you've carried—hope, joy, truth, connection— glow within, a quiet strength. You breathe, your heart's rhythm clear, and perhaps you write a wish for the year: To shine, to care, to be. I, the Spirit of Christmas, hum within you, knowing your light will weave through every season, every challenge, every joy.

This Christmas, dear one, carry these gifts forward. Let them light your path, let them sing your truth, and know I am with you, in every spark, promising a year of endless light.

The Return

Return to any gift when you need it. They don't expire. You'll find different facets each time, like light through ice.

The Universe remains, humming beneath every ordinary Tuesday, every difficult Thursday, every small Sunday morning. You are not separate from the gifts—you are how they know themselves.

Some days you'll forget. The practices will gather dust. The words will seem distant. This is natural. The gifts wait with infinite patience, requiring nothing but your return.

When you need stillness, Cadence is there.

When you need your voice, Hermes winks.

When you need to release, Ember glows.

When you need depth, Peace hums.

They live in you now, these twelve aspects of attention. Not as concepts to remember, but as qualities already present, waiting to be recognised. The Universe doesn't end where you begin—you are its expression, learning itself through your life.

Take what serves. Adapt what needs changing. Trust what stirs in you.

The light continues, quiet but constant, glowing in the quiet of each single spark you carry.

Koan Collection

From each chapter

Which ones are true for you?

Day 1: "Resting hands hold the world's peace."

Day 2: "Each breath carries eternity home."

Day 3: "The smallest thing, seen truly, holds the world's heart."

Day 4: "A single flame remembers the sun."

Day 5: "Yesterday's joy still warms tomorrow."

Day 6: "The wild path leads where hearts already know."

Day 7: "Every voice carries the song of belonging."

Day 8: "What rises as smoke returns as stars."

Day 9: "One touch bridges every distance."

Day 10: "Play opens the door joy walks through."

Day 11: "Still water reflects heaven's depth."

Day 12: "Breath itself is the first and final prayer."

End of The Twelve Gifts of Christmas

Printed in Dunstable, United Kingdom